THE STORY OF NELSON MANDELA

A Biography Book for New Readers

— Written by —
Floyd Stokes, LHD

—Illustrated by—
Anastasia Magloire Williams

ROCKRIDGE PRESS

To Ron Claiborne, a huge Nelson Mandela fan. Thank you for your friendship, leadership, and mentorship over the years.

For general information on our other products and services or to obtain technical support, please contact our Customer Care Department within the United States at (866) 744-2665, or outside the United States at (510) 253-0500.

Rockridge Press publishes its books in a variety of electronic and print formats. Some content that appears in print may not be available in electronic books, and vice versa.

Series Designer: Angela Navarra
Interior and Cover Designer: Emma Hall
Art Producer: Sara Feinstein
Editor: Mary Colgan
Production Editor: Jenna Dutton
Production Manager: Martin Worthington

ISBN: Print 978-1-64876-637-4 | eBook 978-1-64876-139-3
R0
Printed in China

CONTENTS

CHAPTER 1

A LEADER IS BORN

Meet Nelson Mandela

Nelson Mandela was born into a royal family of the Thembu people in South Africa. His father, the local chief and advisor to the king, gave him the name Rolihlahla (khol-ee-HLAA-hlaa). In his native language of Xhosa (KOH-sah or HO-sah), the name means "pulling the branch of a tree." But the more common meaning is "troublemaker." Nelson grew up to be a troublemaker in the best way. He made good trouble by fighting against unfair laws. When Nelson was a boy, however, few people would have guessed his future.

South Africa is a country located at the southern tip of the **continent** of Africa. It has beautiful mountains, valleys, deserts, and forests. The country is also rich in natural resources like gold and diamonds. White European settlers came to South Africa in search of these treasures. Over time, they took over the country. The white settlers started separating Black and white people and made laws that restricted Black people's rights.

Nelson dedicated his life to fighting against these unjust laws. The government arrested him and many others for standing up for what they believed in—equal rights for all people. But Nelson never gave up. He went on to become the first Black president of South Africa. He inspired people from around the world and became a symbol of peace and justice. He changed South Africa and the world forever with his work and words.

Nelson's South Africa

Nelson was born in South Africa on July 18, 1918. Long before he was born, Black kings and queens ruled the area. Over hundreds of years, the Dutch, British, and others came to **colonize**, or take over, parts of South Africa. Then, in the late 1800s, something happened that changed South Africa forever: Gold and diamonds were found in the land. No one had known that South Africa had such riches.

MYTH	FACT
White people controlled South Africa because there were more white people than Black people in the country.	White people controlled South Africa because they had more advanced weapons and brought disease to the country, which let them gain more power.

JUMP -IN THE- THINK TANK

Nelson's father gave him his birth name, which means "troublemaker." Do you know who chose your name? Does it have a meaning?

White Europeans seeking fortune flooded the country. They brought powerful weapons with them. They also brought new diseases. The Africans' **immune systems** had no defense against these diseases. Many people died.

Over time, these **colonists** gained more and more control of the country. Black South Africans

were sold into **slavery** and shipped to Europe and America. The ones who stayed were robbed of their land, animals, and jobs. Even though there were many more Black people than white people, whites had almost all of the power. Whites made laws about where Black people could live and go to school. South African men had to leave their families to work in the gold and diamond mines. People were unhappy and afraid. It was a perfect time for an **inspiring** leader to rise up.

Diamonds are found in South Africa.

Nelson Mandela is born.

1867 **1918** **WHEN?**

CHAPTER 2

THE EARLY YEARS

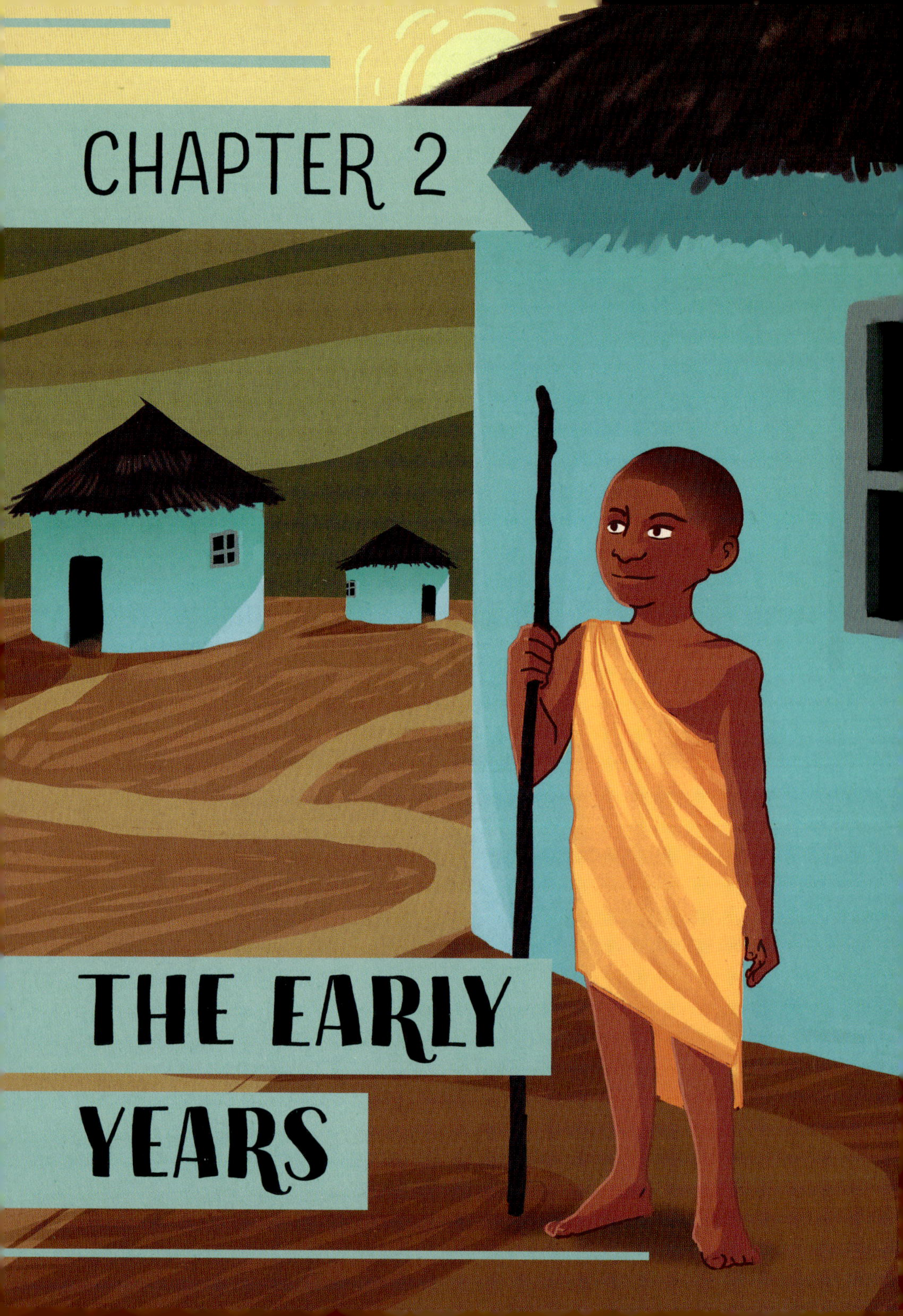

Growing Up

Nelson was born in a mud hut in the tiny village of Mvezo (m-VEE-zo). His father, Gadla, was a chief of the Thembu royal family. In their religion, men could have more than one wife. Nelson's mother, Nosekeni, was one of his father's four wives.

When Nelson was still a baby, his father got in trouble for standing up to an unfair British judge. The judge took away his position as chief. He also took away most of his money, land, and animals. The family could no longer afford to live in Mvezo. Nelson's mother took him and his three little sisters to live with her family in the nearby village of Qunu (KOO-noo).

In Qunu, families lived in small huts shaped like beehives. The huts had mud walls and a wooden pole through the middle to hold up the grass roofs. Nelson had a happy life in Qunu. He learned how to herd sheep and cattle by the time he was five years old. He and the other children made their own toys, hunted small animals, and practiced fighting with sticks. Nelson loved being outdoors.

When Nelson was seven, his mother sent him to a school run by Christian teachers. He was the first person in his family to go to school. His family had no money for new clothes. Like other children in his village, Nelson wore a blanket dyed with red clay most days. His father cut off a pair of his own pants at the knee so they were short enough for Nelson. Nelson proudly walked to school in his new pants. He was given the name Nelson the same day. At the time, it was **tradition** that Christian teachers would give students English names.

Great Place

Sadly, Nelson's father died when Nelson was 12 years old. Nelson's mother was forced to make a difficult decision. She sent Nelson to live with his uncle, Chief Jongintaba (JOHN-geen-taa-baa). His mother knew that the chief could take better care of him.

The Mandela Family Tree

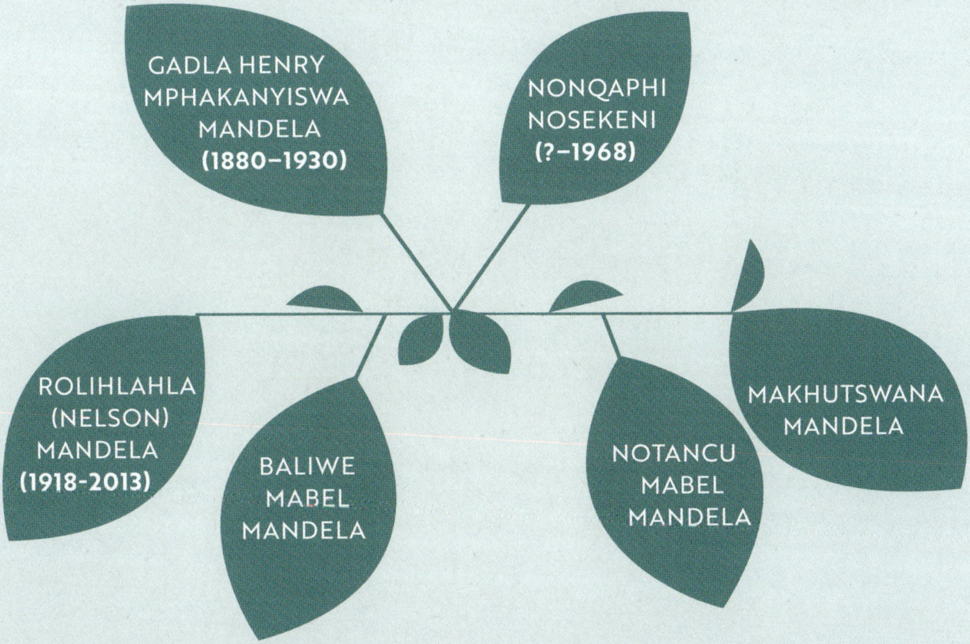

Nelson's heart sank as he walked away from Qunu and all the happy memories he had made there.

The chief's home was called the Great Place. It was made up of several buildings surrounded by gardens and fruit trees. Nelson had never seen anything so grand. He felt like he was entering a magical kingdom.

The chief and his wife welcomed Nelson into their lives. They sent him to school and treated him the same as their own son, Justice. Justice was four years older than Nelson. The two boys became close friends. Sometimes the chief allowed them to race horses. On some nights, Nelson and the other boys would dance while the girls sang and clapped. Nelson missed his mother, but he was happy with his new life.

JUMP IN THE THINK TANK

Nelson was sad to move away from Qunu. Why do you think it can be difficult to move to another home? What good things might come from moving?

> "Education is the most powerful weapon which you can use to change the world."

Nelson learned a lot about **leadership** while living at the Great Place, as his uncle was preparing him to become a royal advisor.

Chief Jongintaba let him come to meetings he held with Thembu **elders**. Nelson would join the men as they gathered around the fireplace. He watched how his uncle treated people who came to him with problems. His uncle would listen to everyone before he made a decision. Every person at the meeting had a voice. These lessons stayed with Nelson for the rest of his life.

WHEN?

1925: Nelson starts school.

1930: Nelson's father dies, and Nelson moves to the Great Place.

CHAPTER 3
BECOMING POLITICAL

Fort Hare

Nelson studied hard as he grew up. He believed that education was his key to a successful life. In 1939, he arrived at the University College of Fort Hare. It was the only all-Black college in South Africa. Only the best students were accepted. At Fort Hare, he met a student named Oliver Tambo. The two became lifelong friends. Years later, they also became law partners.

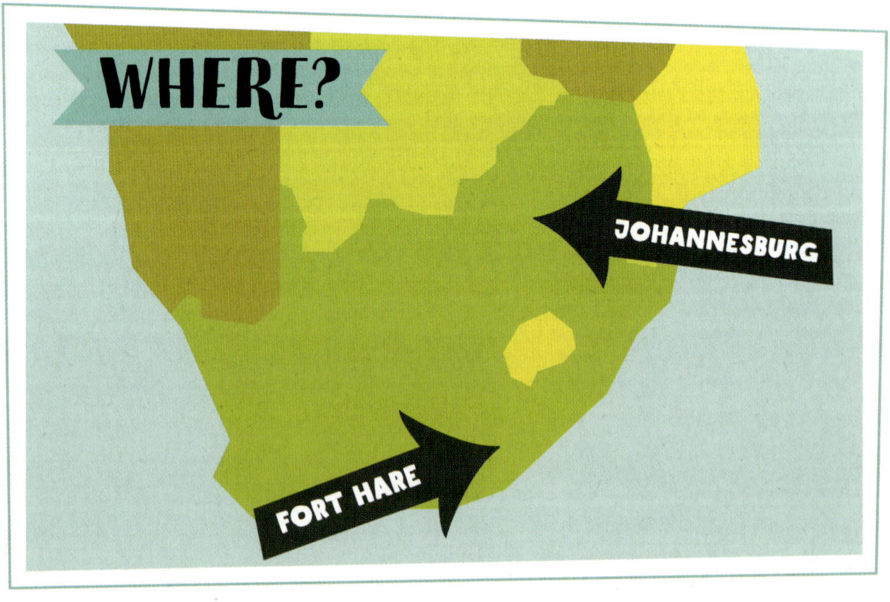

Nelson started to compete in soccer, running, and boxing. He practiced ballroom dancing. He even acted in a play! He also became interested in **politics**. He hoped to work for the government after college. This would be an important job. He would be able to buy a new house for his mother and make her life easier. In his second year of college, he was **nominated** for student government. The students wanted better food. They also wanted a stronger voice in school policies. The school refused to do what they asked. Nelson quit the student government in **protest**. Like his father had when he stood up to the unfair judge, Nelson paid a price for standing up for his beliefs: He was expelled from Fort Hare. Nelson was upset to be kicked out.

He worried he was throwing away his dreams. But he also felt proud that he had stood by the other students.

Chief Jongintaba was angry and disappointed when Nelson left college. The chief was very sick. He was worried about what would happen to Nelson and Justice in the future. He chose brides for the two young men and told them they must get married right away. Neither Nelson nor Justice was ready for marriage. They ran away to Johannesburg, the biggest city in South Africa. Justice soon went back, but Nelson convinced the chief to let him stay. He was ready for an **independent** life.

Life in Johannesburg

Johannesburg was a whole new world for Nelson. He rented a room in the Alexandra township, a very poor neighborhood that was sometimes called "Dark City" because it didn't have electricity.

This was because the white city managers would not let Alexandra collect taxes to manage the area. Nelson soon saw that life in the city was very bad for Black people. They mostly worked in the gold and diamond mines, which were low-paying jobs. Whites held all the good jobs. They ran the government and were getting rich from owning the mines. And Black people were not allowed to move freely through the city. They were forced to live in areas like Alexandra, which didn't have any of the resources that white parts of the city did.

JUMP IN THE THINK TANK

Nelson quit student government even though he knew he would be punished. Do you think he did the right thing?

In Johannesburg, Nelson met a businessman named Walter Sisulu. The two men were instantly impressed with each other. Nelson admired how well Walter spoke English. Walter thought Nelson was a born leader.

He helped Nelson get a job as a law clerk. This was a big break for Nelson. White law firms did not usually hire Black clerks. Nelson also took college classes by mail. He worked during the day and studied at night. In 1942, Nelson earned his bachelor's degree from the University of South Africa. Shortly after graduation, Walter introduced Nelson to his cousin, Evelyn Mase. Nelson immediately asked her on a date.

MYTH &	FACT
Everyone could live anywhere they wanted in Johannesburg.	Black people were forced to live in poor, dirty parts of the city that didn't get the same resources white areas did.

The two quickly fell in love. Before long, they were married.

In 1942, Nelson joined the African National Congress (ANC). The ANC worked for equal rights for Black South Africans. Their meetings were filled with lively **debate** about issues affecting Black people. Nelson was inspired by their passion. However, he and other young men in the ANC started to feel that things weren't changing fast enough. In 1944, they started the ANC Youth League. Nelson had become a true **activist**!

WHEN?

1939 Nelson starts college at University College of Fort Hare.

1940 Nelson is expelled.

1941 Nelson and Justice move to Johannesburg.

1942 Nelson joins the ANC.

1944 Nelson marries Evelyn Mase and helps found the ANC Youth League.

CHAPTER 4

CIVIL RIGHTS ACTIVIST

Apartheid

Nelson and Evelyn had four children. Sadly, one daughter died when she was only a baby. Nelson loved spending time with his family. He loved playing with his children, reading to them at bedtime, and relaxing at home. But Nelson also cared deeply about what was happening in the country. His work often took him away from his family.

The all-white National Party was voted into power in 1948. They began a policy called **apartheid**. Apartheid means "apartness" in the **Afrikaans** language. The National Party believed Blacks were **inferior** to whites. They passed cruel laws to keep themselves in power. Black people couldn't vote. People of different races couldn't get married, ride on buses together, or even live in the same neighborhood. Perhaps worst of all, Black people had to carry **passbooks** at all times. Passbooks had a person's name and picture and also information such as where they were allowed to work and travel. If a Black person was caught without their passbook, they could be arrested.

After seeing the terrible things the government stood for, Nelson knew he would never work for it like he'd planned. In 1952, he and Oliver Tambo opened the first Black law firm in South Africa. They represented Black people arrested under the new apartheid laws. Few law firms would take Black clients, so lots of people came to their office. Oliver usually

worked in the office while Nelson went to court. He would ignore the rules of apartheid, walking boldly through the "whites only" door at the courthouse. He became a powerful figure in the fight for **equality**. People came to court just to watch him in action.

Protest

In 1952, the ANC decided to take their biggest action yet. They would refuse to follow the apartheid laws, even if it meant they had to go to jail. More than 8,500 people joined the cause, holding peaceful protests all over the country. These protests were small but powerful. Protesters entered train cars and restrooms marked "whites only." They stayed out past **curfew**. They marched together while singing freedom songs. This series of protests was called the Defiance Campaign.

The ANC had told people not to use violence no matter what happened. Protesters knew they might be hurt, but they kept their word. Many, including Nelson, were arrested and beaten. People in government started to see Nelson as a troublemaker, just like his birth name said. Soon he was **banned** from making public speeches. He was not allowed to write for newspapers. He couldn't even leave his neighborhood.

Nelson still refused to back down. He and other activists started working on a **bill of rights** called the Freedom Charter. They wanted fairness and equality for all South Africans. This was the first time that people of different races worked together in South Africa. On June 25 and 26 of 1955, more than 3,000 people from all over the country gathered on a soccer field in Kliptown. This gathering was called the Congress of the People. People

JUMP -IN THE- THINK TANK

What do you think were the advantages of people of different races working together in South Africa?

cheered wildly and shouted "Afrika!" as the charter was read. But then police arrived. The Congress of the People came to an end, but Nelson and the ANC were more determined than ever.

> "We are not in opposition to any government or class of people. We are opposing a system which has for years kept a vast section of the non-European people in bondage."

WHEN?

1948	1952	1955
Apartheid begins.	Nelson and Oliver Tambo open a law practice.	The Congress of the People takes place.

CHAPTER 5

FIGHTING FOR JUSTICE

Treason Trial Years

In the early morning on December 5, 1956, Nelson awoke to loud pounding on his door. The police had come to arrest him and charge him with high **treason**. Nelson and 155 other activists were taken to jail. Conditions there were **dismal**, with bare, concrete cells and thin blankets. But the men were cheered by news from around the world. People were protesting for them! There were also huge crowds rooting for them when they were taken to court. They walked through the doors with their fists held high. The trial lasted more than four years. Finally, all charges against Nelson and the others were dropped.

Nelson did not have to stay in jail during the trial. He was allowed to go home after two weeks. When Nelson entered his house, he found it empty. His wife, Evelyn, had left him. Nelson had known she had not agreed with his work with

the ANC. She did not like that he spent so many hours away from the family. Even so, Nelson was sad and surprised that she had left. What was once a house full of laughing children was now empty and quiet.

In 1957, Nelson saw a beautiful woman at a bus stop. Weeks later, she came into his office for legal help. Her name was Winnie. Nelson fell in love the moment he met her. Winnie was one of the first Black social workers in South Africa. She was smart and **passionate** about politics and the ANC. Nelson and Winnie got married a year later and had two daughters together. Winnie stood by Nelson during his trial. As a couple, they worked together to end apartheid.

Going Underground

On March 21, 1960, a crowd of 10,000 people met at the police station in the township of Sharpeville to protest passbooks. Without warning, the police fired their guns into the crowd. They killed 69 unarmed Black South Africans. Another 180, including 19 children, were badly hurt. People around the world were horrified when they learned what had happened.

> A nation should not be judged by how it treats its highest citizens, but its lowest ones.

The Sharpeville **massacre** changed how Nelson thought about ending apartheid. He no longer felt that peaceful protests would be enough. He helped start a group called Spear of the Nation. The group did not want to hurt anyone. They wanted to get people's attention by **disrupting** the country. Their plan was to set off homemade bombs at power plants and government offices when people were not in the buildings.

JUMP IN THE THINK TANK

Why do you think people protest? Do you know of any protests happening now?

After Sharpeville, the government declared a state of emergency. People were not allowed to gather in public. The police could arrest and hold anyone, even without proof of a crime. Nelson and others burned their passbooks in protest. The police raided Nelson's home and arrested him, leaving Winnie, who was pregnant, by herself.

After Nelson was released from jail, the police watched his house day and night. It was no longer safe for him there. He was forced to leave his family and go into hiding. He hid at various **safe houses** and even traveled outside the country to gather more support for the ANC. While in South Africa, Nelson often wore disguises to hide from police. He let his hair and his beard grow long and would dress as a chef or a driver or a field worker. He narrowly escaped many times. Finally, on August 5, 1962, the police caught up with him. He was dressed as a driver, but the police had known he was coming and this time they were not fooled.

WHEN?

1960	1961	1962
The Sharpeville Massacre takes place.	Nelson goes into hiding.	Nelson is arrested.

CHAPTER 6

PRISON YEARS

Robben Island

Nelson was put on trial again. In April 1964, he gave a three-hour speech in court, spreading his message about the unfairness of apartheid. He did not deny that he had broken laws, but he explained why he had done so. The courthouse was silent as he spoke. Some people were brought to tears. Two months later, he was found guilty and sentenced to life in prison.

In June 1964, Nelson was sent to Robben Island prison. It was damp and horribly cold on the island, but prisoners were dressed in short pants and shoes without socks. Nelson's jail cell was eight feet by seven feet with a mat on the floor for sleeping. He was given a bucket to use as a toilet.

While he was in prison, Nelson had very little contact with the outside world. He was allowed only two visitors and could write only two letters per year. Prisoners were not allowed to read newspapers, but sometimes guards would give them news, especially news that would upset them. Nelson learned that his wife, Winnie, had been arrested from a newspaper clipping left by a guard.

Nelson tried to make the best of his time in prison. He read and studied as often as he could. He exercised every morning, running in place and doing push-ups in his jail

cell. He and other prisoners found creative ways to talk to each other. They hid notes under piles of dirty dishes or inside old matchbooks. Nelson even found a way to write! He secretly wrote much of his autobiography, *Long Walk to Freedom*, during those lonely years.

> I have cherished the ideal of a democratic and free society in which all persons live together in harmony and with equal opportunities.

Free Mandela!

Outside of the prison, Black South Africans continued to struggle against apartheid. The unrest that spread across the country couldn't be bottled up again. Oliver Tambo refused to let people forget Nelson. In 1980, he started the "Free Nelson Mandela" campaign. Mayors from 20,000 cities on every continent signed a document demanding Nelson's freedom. Even though he was out of sight, Nelson was still the face of the anti-apartheid movement.

In 1982, after 18 years on Robben Island, Nelson was moved to Pollsmoor Prison. At Pollsmoor, prisoners had real beds and toilets, and better meals. Even though he was more comfortable, Nelson wondered why he had been moved. He thought the government might be trying to take away his power by splitting him up from his friends.

In 1985, the South African prime minister, P. W. Botha, offered Nelson a deal. He would release Nelson from prison if Nelson said it was wrong to use violence in protest.

Nelson did not accept. Instead, he secretly wrote a speech about the offer. He wrote that he had tried peaceful protest, but had been met with violence. He wrote that even if he were freed from prison, he could not be free in a country where he could not vote. His daughter Zindzi read the inspiring speech to a packed stadium. The crowd cheered when she finished.

F. W. de Klerk became president of South Africa in 1989. He believed that apartheid needed to end.

JUMP —IN THE— THINK TANK

Nelson's daughter read his speech encouraging the people and rejecting the prime minister's offer. How do you think she felt doing this? How would you feel?

> "Honor belongs to those who never forsake the truth even when things seem dark and grim."

He started to make changes, like lifting the ban on the ANC. He also made another big decision: to free Nelson Mandela! On February 11, 1990—after 27 years behind bars—Nelson left prison as a free man at the age of 71. He and Winnie walked through the prison gate together. They were greeted by a huge crowd celebrating Nelson's release.

WHEN?

Nelson is sent to Robben Island prison.

1964

Oliver Tambo starts "Free Mandela" campaign.

1980

Nelson is moved to Pollsmoor Prison.

1982

Nelson rejects P. W. Botha's offer to be released.

1985

Nelson is freed from prison after 27 years.

1990

CHAPTER 7
WORLD LEADER

President Mandela

Nelson quickly got back to work with the ANC. He wanted the world to see that his time in prison had not taken away his spirit or his drive for change. The country was still very divided. Many white people still believed in apartheid. Many Black people felt that things were changing too slowly. Nelson and the ANC often met with President de Klerk and others in the government. In 1992, they signed a Record of Understanding. This agreement laid out a plan to transition to a new government. In 1993, Nelson and President de Klerk were jointly awarded the **Nobel Peace Prize** for their efforts in bringing the country together.

In late April 1994, Nelson ran against President de Klerk in South Africa's first **democratic** election. For the first time, South Africans of every race could vote. The country was alive with hope and excitement.

People stood in line for hours, patiently waiting to vote. When all the votes were counted, the ANC party won with 62 percent of the vote. Nelson Mandela became the first Black president of South Africa! When Nelson was sworn in, a billion people around the world watched on television.

As President, Nelson followed the example he had learned from Chief Jongintaba. He listened to all parties and found things most people could agree on. He worked with the different groups to create a new **constitution**, which was adopted in 1996. Nelson believed that forgiveness was the way forward for South Africa and he spread this message to the people. He even forgave those who had put him in prison for all those years.

Madiba

Nelson decided to serve only one term as president. He believed it was time for a younger person to lead, so he stepped down in June 1999. In 2005, Nelson's son Makgatho died of AIDS, a disease that attacks the immune system. Nelson then committed himself to teaching South Africans about the disease. His work helped save millions of lives. Nelson also finally had time to do things that he missed while in prison. He and Winnie had divorced and he had married Graca Machel, a children's rights activist, in 1998.

MYTH & FACT

MYTH: All South Africans loved and agreed with Nelson Mandela.

FACT: Some thought he should have done more for Black South Africans and to punish whites who killed people and took land away.

JUMP -IN THE- THINK TANK

Why do you think Nelson forgave the people who put him in jail? Do you think forgiveness is important? Why?

Together with Graca, he spent holidays, birthdays, graduations, and weddings with his family.

Today, when South Africans think of Nelson, they use the word "Madiba." The term is an **endearment** that means "father." In 2009, the United Nations declared Nelson's birthday, July 18, as Nelson Mandela

> "A winner is a dreamer who never gives up."

International Day, a day meant for volunteering and community service.

The world mourned when Nelson Mandela passed away on December 5, 2013, at the age of 95. His vision of a peaceful and fair world with equality for all lives on through his legacy.

WHEN?

1993 — Nelson and President de Klerk win the Nobel Peace Prize.

1994 — Nelson is elected president of South Africa.

1996 — Constitution of the Republic of South Africa is adopted.

1999 — Nelson steps down from presidency after one term.

2013 — Nelson passes away on December 5.

CHAPTER 8

SO . . . WHO WAS NELSON MANDELA ?

Challenge Accepted!

Now that you have learned all about Nelson Mandela's amazing life, let's test your new knowledge with a little who, what, when, where, why, and how quiz. Feel free to look back in the book to find the answers if you need to, but try to remember first!

1 What does Nelson's birth name, Rolihlahla, mean?

- A Troublemaker
- B Warrior
- C Shepherd
- D King

2 Where was Nelson born?

- A United States
- B South Africa
- C France
- D Australia

3 Who gave Nelson his English name?

→ A His mother

→ B His father

→ C His teacher

→ D His uncle

4 Under apartheid, which of these was against the law for Black people?

→ A Voting

→ B Going out without a passbook

→ C Marrying a white person

→ D All of the above

5 How many years did Nelson spend in prison?

→ A 5 years

→ B 20 years

→ C 27 years

→ D 33 years

6 **What is one of the sports Nelson played in college?**

→ A Boxing

→ B Swimming

→ C Baseball

→ D Basketball

7 **When did Nelson become president?**

→ A 1960

→ B 1976

→ C 1982

→ D 1994

8 **How did Nelson make history?**

→ A He discovered gold and diamonds in South Africa.

→ B He became chief of the Thembu tribe.

→ C He was South Africa's first Black president.

→ D He started the African National Congress.

9 Who freed Nelson from prison?

- A Desmond Tutu
- B F. W. de Klerk
- C John F. Kennedy
- D Abraham Lincoln

10 Why did Nelson become an activist?

- A He wanted equal rights for all people.
- B He wanted to be president.
- C He wanted the Nobel Peace Prize.
- D He wanted to be famous.

Answers: 1. A; 2. B; 3. C; 4. D; 5. C; 6. A; 7. D; 8. C; 9. B; 10. A

Our World

Nelson Mandela broke many barriers in his fight for equal rights. Let's look at some of the ways his legacy lives on today.

→ Nelson's fight against apartheid inspired Dr. Martin Luther King Jr. and many others during the civil rights movement in the United States. His influence went much further than South Africa. His work helped people around the world fight for equal rights.

→ Nelson became South Africa's first Black president. He showed Black people in South Africa and around the world that they could achieve things that once seemed impossible. He continues to be a source of hope and inspiration for people of all races.

→ Nelson fought for children. He started the Nelson Mandela Children's Fund to fight poverty, hunger, and homelessness and improve life for South African children. The institute is still working to help children today.

JUMP IN THE THINK TANK FOR MORE!

Can you think of other lessons we can learn from Nelson's life? Think about these questions to keep exploring!

→ For more than 30 years, Nelson fought for justice for all people. Do you think he ever wanted to give up? What do you think kept him going?

→ Many people saw Nelson as a good leader. What do you think it means to be a good leader? Can you think of any leaders in your life? What do they have in common?

→ Nelson was the first Black president in South Africa. What might be hard about being first at something?

Glossary

activist: A person who works to bring about change for something they care very much about

Afrikaans: A language that evolved from Dutch and is spoken in South Africa

apartheid: A system for keeping people separated by race

banned: Not allowed by law

bill of rights: A document outlining the basic rights of all people

colonists: People who live in a colony

colonize: When people go to a foreign country to claim the land as their own, forming a colony

constitution: A set of rules that states how a country is run

continent: One of the seven large areas of land on Earth

curfew: A rule stating what time people need to be home or off the streets

debate: An argument about a specific topic

democratic: Relating to democracy, a form of government in which people have a say in how their government is run

dismal: Gloomy or unhappy

disrupting: Interrupting by causing disorder and confusion

elders: People who have authority because of their age and experience

endearment: A word that expresses love or affection

equality: When every person in a group has the same rights and opportunities

immune system: The system that helps your body fight off sickness

independent: Free from the control of another

inferior: Less important or valuable

inspiring: Causing other people to feel hopeful

leadership: Ability to lead

massacre: An act of cruelty that kills many people

Nobel Peace Prize: An important award given to a person or people who have worked to encourage peace

nominated: Suggested as the possible winner of an award or prize

passbook: A form of identification that Black people had to carry with them at all times during apartheid

passionate: Showing strong feeling or emotion

politics: Activities related to the government of a city, state, country, or nation

protest: The act of showing that you disagree with something

safe house: A place where someone can hide from danger or be protected

slavery: A system in which a person is owned by another person or people; a slave is considered by law as property and does not have the rights held by free people

tradition: Belief or activity in a culture or custom that continues from one generation to the next

treason: An attempt to overthrow the government

Bibliography

Books

Nelson, Kadir. *Nelson Mandela*. New York: Katherine Tegen Books, 2013.

Mandela, Nelson Rolihlahla. *Long Walk to Freedom: The Autobiography of Nelson Mandela*. New York: Little, Brown & Company, 1994.

Website

Nelson Mandela Foundation: NelsonMandela.org

Acknowledgments

The legacy of Nelson Mandela is an awe-inspiring one. Growing up in the Deep South of Mississippi we learned of Nelson Mandela. He was an inspiration then and now. Special thanks to my mom, Florence. Thank you for loving me, believing in me, and sacrificing for me. To Wayne, Niecy, Dev, Madi, and Livie, for being the best children a man could have. To everyone who supported me and purchased my books. You have helped me greatly in getting to this point. To my friend Ron Claiborne, Nelson Mandela's biggest fan. Thank you to my editor, Mary Colgan, and the entire Callisto team.

About the Author

FLOYD STOKES, LHD, is the founder and executive director of the American Literacy Corporation (ALC), which is a nonprofit organization established in August 2000 that promotes reading to children. He is the author of more than 20 children's books. Floyd is the recipient of several awards, including the James Patterson PageTurner Award, and his high school renamed their library in his honor. Floyd has read to children in all 50 states. He lives in Harrisburg, Pennsylvania. Learn more about his work at SuperReader.org.

About the Illustrator

ANASTASIA MAGLOIRE WILLIAMS is an illustrator, storyteller, and designer based in sunny Florida. She enjoys working with bright colors, bold shapes, and vibrant stories that reflect a diverse and beautiful world. When she isn't reading everything in sight, Ana can be found tending to her growing number of plants, gaming with friends, and putting extra cheese on everything.

WHO WILL INSPIRE YOU NEXT?

EXPLORE A WORLD OF HEROES AND ROLE MODELS IN ***THE STORY OF***... BIOGRAPHY SERIES FOR NEW READERS.

LOOK FOR THIS SERIES
WHEREVER BOOKS AND EBOOKS ARE SOLD

Alexander Hamilton
Albert Einstein
Martin Luther King Jr.
George Washington
Jane Goodall
Ruth Bader Ginsburg
Helen Keller
Marie Curie